EXPOSED NERVES

Published by Raw Dog Screaming Press
Bowie, MD

First Edition

Book design: Jennifer Barnes

egolikeness.com

Printed in the United States of America
ISBN: 978-1-947879-36-2

Library of Congress Control Number:
9781947879362

www.RawDogScreaming.com

EXPOSED NERVES

by Lucy A. Snyder

Table of Contents

Exposure: A Foreword

by Mary A. Turzillo

Exposed Nerves vibrates with energy and rewards with clarity of vision.

"My power animal is the oyster," Lucy Snyder tells us, in a December 17, 2007 interview for *GUD*. And what a power animal it is! The oyster that Snyder slyly refers to as an unlikely muse creates a jewel, a thing of beauty and value from an irritant, a goad that causes her, as a master poet, to sing out. In this superb collection, she exposes social hypocrisy and vanity, but in a way that enlightens. Acts of injustice and attitudes of oppression are motes of grit that generate striking poetic pearls.

Some of the irritants in *Exposed Nerves* include warped romance, the inequities of the American health system, racist hypocrisy, diminution of anybody who is different, and misogyny both in politics and in the intimate realm.

In *Exposed Nerves*, romantic relationships turn political. Snyder pillories misogyny and male chauvinism in her opening poem, "The Scientist's Paramour." Thus this uniquely satisfying collection begins with a betrayal: the calf not realizing he is about to become veal; the stag beetle (Lucanida) believing itself to be adored before being collected (some rare specimens can fetch up to $600 on eBay), and the scientist's paramour realizing she has also been collected.

While many of her poems can be seen as social commentary or protest, Snyder also identifies as a horror writer, explaining her adoption of that genre in "Scary." In that poem, a teenage persona comforts herself by saying "It's more fun to fear fictional monsters" than to face the fear of "the tedious crap of adulthood" and the prospect of the "stinking welter of failure."

Then in the very next poem Snyder exemplifies that mode of escapism in "Dangerous," in which a teen is warned against venturing out into the real, social world whereupon he murders his hypocritical compeers and becomes the real danger himself. In "turnt," another escapist nightmare, a girl is lured into a hot session in a car. She, however, becomes the predator. In both these poems, the persona becomes the feared object.

Horror? Social protest? Why not both in the same complex work?

Synder turns her laser eye upon the American health system in the section "You Might Feel a Slight Sting." The title itself is high irony, reminding the reader of Jonathan Swift's remark in *A Tale of a Tub*: "I saw a woman flay'd, and you will hardly believe, how much it alter'd her person for the worse." Ironic understatement of the type Swift used is sprinkled throughout this section, starting with this title.

In "February," Snyder excoriates cancer, but also the horrors that cancer treatment involves. Some of the poem is about the nightmare of the disease itself. But the medical profession is also a target. The phrase "mammary mammogram mammon" suggests that profit may be a latent rationale in the treatment of the disease. "Relax, honey, this'll be quick" stands as a heartlessly insensitive prologue to the ensuing actions, where Snyder tells us of the baldness, the "useless arm numb." the "ulcered tongue," radiation, and pain, and then the names of cancer drugs, which she makes part of the sound effects of the piece. The poem ends with the word "grave." All the pain, mutilation, and sacrifice have been for nothing. This poem sticks with me and makes me shudder; it's one of Snyder's poems I can't get out of my mind.

The drug industry and the American health care system are the targets of protest in "Chronic." A patient's diagnosis comes after thirty fruitless years of doctoring and suffering. But alas, the treatment costs two thousand dollars a day and is not covered by insurance. Too typical! The poem ends with the sardonic, "isn't it wonderful/to finally be vindicated?"

The human condition, the fact of being the victim of savage emotional pain, is spotlighted in "It's Fine." The persona of the poem is reacting to the silliness of a man saying the worst pain he ever experienced was being struck accidentally in the testicles by his own son. The irony of this, to the persona, who has lost a child, is that her own pain, like the man's, has to do with an offspring. And further irony is that it is worse than the man with the living son can imagine.

> The dragon of my grief
> coiled silent inside me
> but I smiled and drank
> fronting proper cheer
> and it was fine
> it was just
> fucking
> fine.

This poem struck me, as a reader, with a profound sense of loss. But I also notice that the bereaved mother expresses her grief as a dragon coiled inside her mind. The dragon is powerful *against* the mother, but it is part of her, and Snyder may be suggesting that the uncoiling is a manifestation of the mother's emotional power. This could even be the power to speak out, as in this poem.

The section called "With Torches" ticks all the hypocrisy boxes. A university (not named, but we could guess) spouts platitudes about diversity, and administrators tsk-tsk about police violence ("a lung hemorrhage after policeman/pulls down her mask to shoot tear gas/directly down her gasping throat") to demonstrators just a few blocks from the U, but don't allow arrests or beatings as an excuse for missing class. Additionally, those in power do not hire people with disabilities or candidates of a different race. And this will not happen until they find "a photogenic morning/person . . . who speaks and thinks just like everyone else."

I'm guessing that "My Neighbor Posts to the Apartment Page" is based on a real incident. A small black woman in her parking lot asks the neighbor for directions or some other kind of help. The neighbor in question does her "civic duty" and calls the police. She then denies any similarity to another incident: "cops shot/some boy playing with a toy," clearly the Tamir Rice killing. As a reader, I want to scream "Karen!" because this is how innocent people are killed. I don't know the outcome of this affair, but the neighbor clearly evinces a racist, even malevolent, intent.

"Lessons," starts with a tender image of a father giving his daughter a grass snake (snakes are frequent in the collection), in order for her to understand that Otherness is not wrong, that even spiders and snakes feel pain. But as the child attends school, she hears boys in her class degrade the Otherness of Blacks by saying they "make great boxers cos they don't feel pain." As if this isn't horrid enough, the teacher "just grinned and switched to math." The evil is systemic; even the educational system endorses monstrous lies.

I could go on and on.

The depictions of hypocrisy are painful to read, and yet, it is by this unmasking that maybe, just maybe, hearts will change. This is the role of protest poetry: to bring the corruption to light. By focusing the poetic camera on it, maybe society can change. Yes, the villagers have torches, but perhaps Snyder's torch is brighter.

Prejudice against additional Otherness is excoriated in "Faith," where a child has been told she is "broken" because of her attraction to other girls. But love makes her realize society's prejudice is wrong, that true faith is rejecting those "pious lies" and living an authentic and vibrant love.

Segueing into Snyder's section called "Final Frontier," hypocrisy in the space program is spotlighted in "When the War Ended" with the lack of recognition of the Black women who, before the advent of modern computers, did all the math that made space flight possible. The poem ends with the irony of Neil Armstrong saying "We come in peace," when Nazi scientists were chosen to forge the moonshot.

The "frontiers" are emotional and social as well as scientific. "Shore Leave," about space explorers or colonists on Mars, laments the wear and tear of age and labor as Martian settlers. The lines "his heart wasn't tall enough/ to see past the barrel of his rocket" makes an anatomical metaphor for sex parts, but may also be a wink at Ray Bradbury's poem about the inadequacy of human power to conquer space: "If We Had Only Taller Been." Maybe the message is that humans don't have the emotional force to sustain space exploration. Or perhaps it is a small, wry tale of romance limping toward extinction under the heavy burden of life on another planet.

Not all of Snyder's work is acerbic; not everything is protest. I fasten upon "Navigational Error" as a specimen of Snyder's playful use of conceit in the sense of extended metaphor. If this poem has a historical ancestor, it would be in the work of John Donne. In this work, a complex extended metaphor compares the turning point (a frontier) of a relationship, the axis of trust and near breakup, to space catastrophes and their avoidance: «you could have left me adrift/in blackout radio silence.» I will leave to the reader the enjoyment of following this extended metaphor, including the burning of the Pistol Star (what a name!), which was once thought to be the most massive star known.

And in fact, the last four poems sing with a positive peace and even joy. In "Dirty Americans," double entendres ("my purple mountain's majesty" and "we'll finally come in peace") season the acerbic social criticism of previous pieces. (Edex, so you won't have to look it up, is an erectile dysfunction drug.)

We also delight in her fascination with serpents, both snakes and dragons, as in "Mythical" about a modern girl Medusa. And let me mention her clever references to pop culture in "Recreation" and "The Disney Gap."

There is so much more! *Exposed Nerves* is a collection that rewards with every poem. I offer my salute to a work that cuts to the heart and yet offers both hope and comfort.

Mary A. Turzillo, Tuesday, April 27, 2021

Part One:
Dark Matter

The Scientist's Paramour

Did the motherless calf fatted in the field
mistake the vet's latex touch for love?
Did the rarest Lucanidae in the forest
see adoration in her collector's gaze?
I can't ask them; the calf is veal,
the bug is pinned under glass.
But I know I saw something
with my beetle-blind eyes.
I'm sure I felt everything
in my dumb meat heart.

Silences

The newborn won't cry
not even after the surgery
to remove its rotting twin.
Unmade parents lying awake,
3am, exhausted in the dark.
The father's quiet dressing,
slipping out into the cold grey
dawn, destination unknown,
too dazed to make a hard turn.
The soft November snowfall
blanketing the overturned car.
Fifteen frantic texts unseen,
muted in a red-soaked coat.

Fragile

H1N1 is such a tiny thing
a wee spiked ball slipping
quietly into cells to sabotage
our sticky machinery. Heat
kills it, alcohol too. It's hard
to imagine this slight particle
stirs so fierce a cellular storm,
wreaks such expensive misery,
clogs lungs, stops hearts, slaying
blooming youths and aged abuelas
faster than the cruelest brutal army.

Scary

There are a trillion things about being teen
to scare the devil out of you. Or maybe *in*.
It's basic: TV people say this must be your best
time ever, but these months are lumps of misery
in a gruel of boredom. And a queasy terror
that TV might be right: life won't get better.

It's scary, so scary out there.

You can't stop puzzling grim possibilities,
turning the future over like a cube to solve:
What if all the tedious crap of adulthood
is a burden that breaks you like a straw?
What if you sprint to meet your dreams
but crash in a stinking welter of failure?
What if nobody ever really loves you
so you die alone, broke, old, forgotten?

It's scary, so scary out there.

It's more fun to fear fictional monsters:
possessive devils, snap-jawed aliens,
howling wolves, snarling madmen,
ravenous dead, tentacled abominations.
Cue up the movie, crack open the book
Gasp and shriek and forget the world.

It's scary, so scary out there.

Dangerous

"Oh, Johnny, it's dangerous outside," Mama cried
When good friends tried to take you caroling one December.
"Just stay in here where you'll be safe and dry."

You couldn't wait to ditch her drab little town when she died,
Tried to forget her in that coffin, but still you remembered:
"Oh, Johnny, it's dangerous outside," Mama cried.

Nobody in the city would hire a kid, no matter how you tried
Homeless, shamefaced, you panhandled, growing thinner
Hitched back to her old house; at least it seemed safe and dry.

The floor is warped, the windows crawling with flies
And their relentless buzz calls you a loser, a sinner.
"Oh, Johnny, it's dangerous outside," Mama cried.

You tried to visit your good friends but they'd always hide,
Whispering, pretending you were nothing but a ragged stranger.
You burned when you spied them at the prom, so safe and dry.

Dogs found their bones in the woods; you weren't tried.
You rock yourself in her rotting house, mind an ember.
"Oh, Johnny, it's dangerous outside," Mama cries.
"Just stay in here where you'll be safe and dry."

turnt

let's get turnt, says the heartbreaking boy
i wanna get crazy, lose my mind tonight
smile, girl, shake what ya mama gave ya

the stereo rattles his Kia's tinted windows
hungry, you shake your head, say it's late
but he grabs your wrist: *just one drink?*

his Marlboro's burnt down to the filter
he's sweating smoke and his whiskey
smells so sweet. you take a long draw

he says *whoa girl you got a hollow leg*
and your heart is pounding skin itching
ancient genes singing pupils constricting

he says *hey that cost me twenty, ease up!*
but you know drink's not your demon tonight
it's the only solution to snuff your appetite

but your cheap date's pulled the bottle away
you're still so famished you can't even think
and before you can say *Stop* you're turning

pulse hammering inside the secluded car
skin splitting over hairy muscle, scarlet claws
and he's screaming, wailing like he's burning

your mind's an ancient void of rage, need,
and this boy you hoped to please is meat.
booming bass muffles the crack of bone

conscience returns; you see what you've done
stare at sticky hands, know you have to move
again. avoid boys, endure your life alone.

it's dark outside; the night's your mother
shielding you, soothing your shame
so you quietly walk yourself home.

The Unforgiving King

My soul needs solace
after thirteen autumn nights
dreaming in yellow.

In St. Barnabé
the organ blows a strange chord
and my heart shudders.

Regal steps echo
across consecrated stone.
The flap of tatters

turns my flesh to gel
so I pray, avert my gaze,
but it's much too late.

Trapped in His shadow,
I plead as He speaks my name
and my world goes dark.

I awake weeping
under a bone white sky streaked
with blood moons, black stars.

I know, marrow deep,
I shall die as twin suns rise
lost in Carcosa.

bad night

the adhesive heat
the startling awake
over and over and
your id drags out
funhouse mirrors
from which bosses
and former besties
snarl how low you
are

at migraine dawn
you wake on bare
mattress, bedclothes
hiding twixt boxspring
and blind blond wall

even the sheets
can't stand you

The Wrong Daughter

Those two redheaded cousins down
in the holler maybe shared a daddy
or maybe nothing but the same bad taste
in dirty boots and boys with boosted cars.

Strangers argue but can't tell 'em apart.
Sometimes their own mamas mistake
Patsy for Addie at a squinting distance,
calling the wrong daughter to dinner.

But she ain't hungry; her mind is racing
burning neural blacktop day and night
nightmares spilling like sludgy motor oil
across the leather of her cracking soul.

The drive-in behind her eyes replays
the same grindhouse flick over and over.
Did relentless twitches put her in danger
or did hairy escapes give her the shakes?

Chicken and eggs are a scorchy mess
in her stepdaddy's red-hot iron skillet
and the slender man growls *Goddammit*
I'll give you something to cry about.

Wolf Waltz

"It's not kind," Red said
as she swung the cellar door
open to coal below. "It's not kind

to play with human hearts."
I wondered if her caution
was a mantra for herself

as if I still had fangs
as if she hadn't wrapped
sheep flay 'round my face.

"Watch out!" she shouted
"Those stairs won't hold!"
a moment before her shove

sent me tumbling, breaking
through every splintering
filthy rusted nail bristling

skin-ripping cracked board.
Yes, I thought, as my heart
spilled across the sooty floor,

yes, a sharp call:
it's not kind
not kind at all.

Employee Recognition Day

At the company picnic
the employees stick
with their cubemates
standing in buffalo circles

because there's a rumor:
a day-shifting werewolf
lurks amongst them
hiding manicured claws.

Is it the admin assistant
whose teeth are too white?
Or that guy in tech support
who smells like raw meat?

The employees fearfully
nibble free hamburgers
as managerial vampires
twirl sympathetic parasols.

Cowboy Shot

The new pornographer
had an old problem:
what to do with
his lead actor's feet?

Her feet were fine:
buffed, lovely heels
pearly nails. The fans
all loved her long toes.

His hooves were okay,
(if you were into that)
but naked feet are weak
and his actors were tough,

American, wholly masculine.
So they tried sneakers, loafers,
cowboy kickers, combat boots
with and without a dozen socks.

But the actor simply looked silly
in nothing but shoes and a hardon.
So the intrepid director rediscovered
that classic frame: mid-thigh to head,

the focus on his rugged face
or his legendary gun. Leave
the parts that do the heavy lifting
to the viewer's limping imagination.

Recreation

We would be two larks winging
our way through the Master's
best, you said. I'd be your Grace
Kelly, your Audrey. Your eager eye
documenting our recreation, old-style
eight-millimeter, hand-cranked.

I don't remember Grant getting naked
as he fled the marauding sky, flat
fields, drab motels, but a true auteur
is no script-slave. Spellbound, I shed
my retro dress, hit the marks you ordered,
amateur heart fluttering in its dark cage.

But you've stopped wearing your tie,
your ring. You've switched to digital
video, the cost of the darkroom too dear.
The trunk of your old green Ford is filled:
coils of rope and plastic sheets. The shower
scene is tomorrow, you smile. I'm silent,
skull-rehearsing my own altered script
as I lie beside you in the feather bed.

The Invisible Woman

co-written with Gary A. Braunbeck

do you really love
this movie? do you
see it in your dreams?

can you dissect its story perfectly
without parroting that article
from an old horror magazine?

can you sit in the dark
again and again with the
veins of its cold silver light
bleeding across the screen?

do you really love this movie
or is it just something to talk about
years afterward
when your grandkids
find it on late-night TV?

can you find yourself
here? are you running
through the big crowd scene,
the one where you're fleeing
angry villagers with torches?

or are you in the unfocused
background of the monster's
tragic life?

could you rise like a firebird
from the cutting room floor
and say *not this time*
not again
I will make you see me
I will not be ignored

Salty

Despite what you said, my love,
you only want pale saccharine
magic: a Splenda Glenda

with cheesecake frosting.
Wave your gourmand wand
and she'll be your candyland.

You crave sweet maiden,
not seasoned mother,
never bitter crone.

My saltiness is legend.
I'm no marshmallow
though I certainly burn.

So, baby, just for you: I'll embody
witchy clichés. Skunk your beer.
Wilt your soufflés. Sour your balls.

I hear that tears pair well with crow.
I'll take my broom and cauldron
and sweep away to Avalon.

A Dream of You

I was in our old home
and you were there
in your favorite chair
full of chat and cheer
petting your favorite cat
and I knew full well
you'd both been dead
for a long fifteen years
so I asked, obliquely,
about your diagnosis.
And you said, "Oh, let's
not talk about that;
you know how upset
your father can get."

But I was the fragile
one: I watched my hands
flake apart like asbestos
in some spectral wind
and you said, "Keep smiling!"
but my bones were crumbling,
body collapsing into a void.
You blankly watched me fall apart
as I struggled without lungs to ask,
Dear God, what are you?

I woke freezing
in sweaty sheets
nerves humming
like plucked strings.

Part Two:
You Might Feel A
Slight Sting

It Only Hurts When I Dream

I tumbled down concrete stairs
in college. Now, a lumpy place
along my spine always aches
when the temperature drops.

I smashed my bike in traffic,
wracked both knees, but wasn't
crushed by cars. When it's warm
they crackle like rice cereal.

But ever since I lost you
I cannot pack that wound;
your absence will forever
hurt. Time heals nothing.

January

The year strolled in
not as a chubby tot
gumming a silk sash,
sporting a top hat
but as a gaunt chap
wearing a dark robe,
bearing a sharp scythe.

February

click! click! click! click!
mammary mammogram Mammon
female meat modestly stripped
medical glass manly gods
little tin lover boy
    Let's just be friends
snot stomach knot Kleenex
stained slides abnormal tissue
weeping seeping creeping
needle punch gloved fist
KY glazed sweating grunting
    Relax, honey, this'll be quick
viral swarms hard cells violet stains
cold lonely drive useless arm numb
docetaxel paclitaxel cisplatin knife
radiation bald aching radio silence
pain ulcered tongue burnt Valentine
grave.

October

Thirteen years, and still
I miss you more than anything.

If you were here, Henry,
October would be a limitless
expanse of pre-teen Halloween.
I'd help you pick out fat pumpkins
for a messy jack-o-lantern massacre,
our yard a garish Styrofoam graveyard,
a different monster movie every night:
mostly cheese, but the occasional fright.

But you›re not here. You›re nowhere
but in what›s left of my imagination.
I›m the sorriest unmother anyone›s seen:
pushing fifty, binging Count Chocula,
ugly crying to "Dear Winter" on Pandora,
wondering who both of us would have been.

November 9, 2016

In November I did my duty
went off to see the dentist
expecting the status quo:
my teeth would need a cleaning
but they would be in order
just like all the years before.

Dr. Freiheit had bad news:
one of my hardworking molars
had cracked straight to the root
lost its silver lining
and demanded a crown.

I was shocked. Dr. Freiheit said
others would have felt the pain
but my own nerve had failed
to alert me to the fracture
and I had surely swallowed
the toxic metal wad.

Suddenly nothing seemed well.
Was my body poisoned?
Were my nerves diseased?
Would this be the first
of many broken teeth
on the road to infirmity?

Dr. Freiheit raised her light
and smiled sympathetically
told me that these things happen
and we'd deal with it systematically.

It's Fine

Our host asked
the room about
the worst pain
we'd ever
experienced.

And the men
merrily recounted
terrible toothaches
tales of bad tattoos
on skin over bone
and kidney stones
all purely awful
but somehow delightful
after time's anesthesia.

Someone looked at me
and I gave a clipped
three syllable reply:
miscarriage.

There's no brave moral
in my old, frail story.
Three days in darkness
wishing for Percocet
praying for death

feeling every single cell
of a future I wanted badly
bleeding mercilessly away.

The men pretended
I hadn't said a word.
A raconteur took over
grinning about his kid
head-butting his nuts.

Laughter charged in
like brave St. Michael.
The dragon of my grief
coiled silent inside me
but I smiled and drank
fronting proper cheer
and it was fine
it was just
fucking
fine.

Chronic

We know that we said
it was all in your head
in the three long decades
since you took a bad turn
but we've got great news!
They just released a paper:
science completely confirms
you're not a hysterical faker!
The problem lies deep
in your cellular machine
and treatment is indicated.
It's just $1000 a dose
injected twice a day
insurance won't pay
but isn't it wonderful
to finally be vindicated?

A Leggy Bestiary

A millipede is rumored
to have a thousand legs;
a centipede, one hundred.

I've found that an impede
often has four furry limbs,
occasionally two shapely ones.

Low Tea

Silver trays, mayonnaise, gray malaise
soft brie, oolong tea, blue ennui
coffee trolley, melancholy
crustless bread, bony dread
silver trays, mayonnaise, gray malaise.

Exit Signs

We visit Linda
who wants out:
she's tired of being chronic,
tired of low tea, indignity;

she's lived long enough
done most all she wants
and says she'll be dead
on the 29th this month.

We bring her daylilies
to brighten the hospice
and coffee Haagen-Dazs
in case she wants a treat.

After we visit, there's a rock show.
I figured I was getting too old
for campus bars 20 years ago
but they still card me at the door.

The bar is a dive, a firetrap,
but the bands are sublime.
I keep an eye on the exits
in case an amplifier sparks.

These boots weren't made to run;
I'm staying until the music stops
but it's horse sense to plan out
some kind of speedy escape.

Linda B. Munn passed away a day earlier than her prediction on October 28, 2019. Rest in peace, Linda.

Part Three:
With Torches

Imagine My Brain Is Barbados

There's the irresistible force
of a heart-pounding *right now*
always crashing backwards
into a dark, unmoving *not-now*

hard as cold rocks lurking
beneath the surging undertow
dragging all my best intentions
and sinking them in the depths.

And yes, I agree: from the beach
the water looks so calm and clear
perfect for a pleasant evening swim,
waves so gentle a babe could stay afloat.

My grown-up plans are paper boats
and the dopamine-fiending pirates
marauding these frontal lobe coasts
burn every bit of tinder they can find.

And I utterly agree: this could be my Waterloo.
The sea's stupidly cold, but the bonfire's warm
so let's just give those pirates a bit more time;
they're bound to stumble on the treasure soon.

In Spite of It

A friend asked me how
I can still create in the face
of our constant crushing dismay
at seeing women harassed, gaslit,
witchburnt, doxxed, cast aside?

And I replied that I still create
because if I stop ... then what?
I will be miserable. The bullies
and creeps will keep being rotten.
Why *shouldn't* I stick to my keys?

I want you to write, my friend.
If you can't write for pleasure,
I want you to write for spite.

Spill the truth from your fevered head,
and to hell with all the gatekeepers
and all the naysayers who whisper
that your soul's joy is not enough.

And if you can't find that joy,
I want you to attack the page
as if it's been your cruel jailer
for 20 long, hard-labor years
and in the cell you just found
power and freedom in the form
of a nice, sharp, sturdy knife.

(In)Jest

She is completely horrified
by my Facebook joke.
To my eye, that jalapeño
was at most a few Scovilles,
and wasn't sent anywhere
close to her broken bowl
but it burned in her mouth
like bitter habaneros.

I don't think I wrote the thing
that I agree would be so terrible
but I can't deny she is hurting
and I'm willing to be wrong
so I apologize privately,
publicly eat all my words,
but she is furiously horrified
no matter what I do.

I don't know the particulars
of her pain, but it's familiar,
and I don't wish it on anyone.
I try to serve her sympathy
but she knocks that platter
out of my virtual hands
and demands to see
my manager.

My reply unmanaged,
she flees my café
the unwritten promise
to never read my work
crumpled on the table.

Later, I realize it's just
as well. My own pain
has roasted my humor
darker than flame-charred
chipotles, twisted it weird
as a gin & squid ink martini.
I was bound to horrify her
sooner or later. That joke
was sweetness and light
next to the horror I write.

Making Light

Occasionally I find myself
stuck in dreadful conversations
and I just want to sit back,
fix the annoying person
in a cold gravestone stare
put on an Appalachian drawl:
"Y'know, muh great-granddaddy
was a murderer.
I got murderin' genes."

But the worst part is
the history is true.

He shot his wife
for being uppity,
or maybe just
for breathing.

That part is lost,
like my granny
was left and lost,
parentless and penniless
with siblings to feed
so she married young,
clinging to the first
friendly boy who asked.

He died in the Depression
and she was pregnant, 19,
still penniless. Surrendered
my barely-weaned mother
to her dead husband's kin
and they kept her away
claiming my sweet granny
was nothin' but a bad seed.

The second worst thing
was my mother's stunted
fortune: her father's family
was grasping and mean
hiding their heartlessness
behind a Christian façade
of piety and hospitality.

They denied her dreams
raised her on scraps
and made her believe
she was lucky to have them.

My great-grandfather's shotgun blast
sent a shockwave rippling through
all the women who survived him.

Even though
I wasn't born
I can hear it
I can feel it
I can meet
my own
stony gaze
and see it.

And maybe it's a fatal flaw
that I try to make light
of such terrible things
but it was always
our women's training
to pin a cheerful daisy
on every disaster.

And after all,
what else can I do?

Lessons

When I was quite small
my father gave me a grass snake
so I wouldn't be afraid. Explained
why it hadn't any legs or eyelids
why it felt weirdly cool to touch.

In the pecan-shaded backyard
of our classic lowcountry home
he showed me spiders' webs,
told how they combat malaria
and related the tale of Arachne.

The following Charleston summer
the residents threatened to riot.
Father made a righteous show
of sending us to safety upstate
and bought a gun to stand guard.

I was scared. My father told me
the negroes in the city were angry,
violent. Reasonless. He never once
spoke of poverty or police brutality,
the charred crosses in family yards.

Years later, I defended spiders and snakes
to squeamish classmates. Teacher smiled.
Boys argued blood sports. One said, *Blacks
make great boxers cos they don't feel pain.*
Teacher just grinned and switched to math.

And it didn't *seem* right. It didn't *sound* right.
Because I knew that even creeping, simple spiders
react to pain. But I didn't ask, because our teacher
didn't speak, didn't blink, didn't bother to correct
the slander that Black people are literally senseless.

People so casually dismissed as less than the stones
supporting the corners of a supposedly good school.
No doubt someone from that class still believes
the evil myth is true. Silence in the face of lies
shines falsehoods brighter than a library of facts.

The Friend Defense

The worst offense that can befall
an upstanding white American
is not death or taxes, but an
accusation of racism.

You'd think it a truth universally
acknowledged, considering
the great wailing and gnashing
of so many middle-class teeth.

"I have black and Mexican friends!"
they cry. Angrily, tearfully. Nobly
lining up unnamed acquaintances
in the thinnest of thin dark lines

to serve as unpaid human shields.
As if this were a game like Red Rover.
As if their neighbors' and coworkers'
obligatory friendly gestures were more

than simple survival in this pale desert.
Smiling in the face of pain's a dictate
that a black or brown face dare not break
or they'll drown in an ocean of white tears.

As if it were a good character defense
to proudly claim to protect people
who are personally quite useful
but damn all the rest.

My Neighbor Posts to the Apartment Page

I'm writing to say
I saw a stranger
at exactly 6:55 am
in our parking lot.

She was a small black
woman with a red purse.
She had a big silver cell
and was frowning at it.

I locked my Ford's doors
before she even saw me
sitting there, warming
up my car. And then

she came over, flashed
me the phone, tried
to say something over
the noise of the engine.

But I knew it was a trick:
she wanted to take my car!
So I yelled "Go away!"
Shooed her like a stray cat.

She had the nerve
to make a face at me
but she walked off
breath steaming.

I watched her wander,
squinting at apartment
doors, probably scouting
for a burglar boyfriend.

So I did my civic duty,
called the local police
and gave the nice officer
a clear, detailed description.

What? No, she couldn't
have needed directions!
That big fancy phone
(probably stolen)
surely had GPS, Waze.

If the battery was dying
or if her apps froze,
or if her data ran out,
she should have planned
ahead, taken proper steps
to avoid seeming suspicious
to the people who belong here.

I'm entitled to my right
to call the police instead
of listening to the likes of *her*.
I don't care if the cops shot
some boy playing with a toy;

I don't have time to worry
about anyone but myself!

You're the one
who brought race
into this conversation.
You're the racist.
Not me.
Not me.

At the Downtown University (June 1, 2020)

Our department director knows it's critical
to be on the right side of things. History
is happening just a few blocks away;
we can hear the chants while we work
and when the wind blows just so
we catch a whiff of pepper spray.

Each morning of the protests, she's sent
emails full of links to essays on black
history, social justice, racial sensitivity
which we are encouraged to read thoroughly
at our leisure at home or on our lunch break;
living history should not interrupt our work.

"We have a diverse student body," she reminds
us. "It's important to support them during this
incredibly stressful time." She offers no word
on whether students who are arrested or beaten
and miss class as a consequence can be excused.
Presumably, staff and faculty must burn leave,

assuming nobody's blinded by a rubber bullet
or suffers lasting brain damage under a boot
or a lung hemorrhage after a policeman
pulls down her mask to shoot tear gas
directly down her gasping throat.
No word on what happens then.

Our college campus is fully ADA compliant
but somehow, you never see a professor
in a wheelchair, nor a support staff member
with a service dog. Our department's faces
range from pale to golf-tanned. If a furious cop
sends the bravest of us to an unpaid retirement,

there's no word if we'll see a new Black hire
or if that person will find the support to last
longer than a white hire with attention deficit
disorder, or chronic depression or social anxiety,
all of which we're told are protected disabilities
but which somehow always end in an empty chair.

I'm sure that our director will hire a Black instructor
just as soon as she finds one who can hold a mirror
that reflects back the qualities she most values
in herself: a PhD who's a photogenic morning
person, an outgoing able-bodied team player
who speaks and thinks just like everyone else.

My Neighbor Defends Her Champion

How dare you speak
ill of our dead? Our boy
was a real American hero.
He scored more points than
any man alive ever did, so
who cares if some stupid girl
got scored, too? Who cares
if there wasn't just one girl
but an entire team's worth
of women with nightmares?
Our ears are shut; shut your
filthy mouth. He's our hero
and we're raising our beloved
strong sons to be just like him.

(Sis)yphus

Your disbelief is a boulder
you blindly drop in my path:
surely I am wrong
about what I've seen;
surely I am mistaken
about what happens
to me and most women.
I shove your skepticism
up yet another pointless hill
with well-supported statistics,
Pulitzer-grade investigative reports
and heart-wrenching memoirs.
The daily research is exhausting
but I push on, ever hoping
the facts will finally penetrate
your cheerful, willful ignorance
and you will stop treating me
as the unreliable narrator
of my own existence.

Maturity

So many weighty implications
in those four fine syllables:
wisdom beyond one's age
steadfastness, reliability,
poise, sense, sensibility.

What young girl doesn't
dream to be seen as wholly
grown up and graceful?

Being declared mature
first feels like a gold star
of honor. Not a lodestone
dragging her to the dark
waters of enforced silence:
being told it is wisdom
to tolerate grabby hands —
boys can't help themselves,
and men are forever boys
— sensible to stoically bear
slimy remarks, dirty glances.

Maturity promises adult privileges
if only, meanwhile, she's perfect
and perfect girls don't complain
they don't show skin or opinion
they don't raise their voices
and surely never their fists.

It whispers a song of sweet freedom
as it slides on cold iron shackles.

Faith

An entire childhood
being told you're broken
but that you could be whole
if you just cast yourself aside,
hide your secret heart forever,
close your eyes, praise Jesus
loud as a church organ's pipe.

I made love to a preacher's daughter
in the glow of Selene's distant face
worshipped at the altar of her hips
whispered prayers into her neck
and when we awoke we wept
for all the years we'd wasted
for the sake of pious lies.

We were born unbroken and alive
and the next morning we kissed
and swore that we'd survive.

After She Slams the Door Behind Her

I'm certain there's irony afoot
— I can smell the telltale tang.
But the trouble is, this teachable
moment references something
from my first or second season
as a girlfriend (maybe fifth
season at most) and it's not
as if I could sit and binge
on every terrible mistake
I made as a reckless youth
(even if I were that kind
of feckless masochist)
because it's Season 33
and who even knows
which neurons hold
those fateful scenes.

This kind of karma
needs the decency
to strike before
we've turned 43
or we've zero
odds of sussing
what the hell
the take-home
wise life lesson
was supposed
to even be.

Romantic Overture #6

Even when
the roses are dewy
the sheets crisp, cool
the chocolate smooth
and dark as lies

Even when
our days are golden honey
and I believe
all that falls
from your candy apple lips

Even then
I lie silent
on your bed
dreading
the scratching cockroach truth

The Disney Gap

I spent my childhood
dancing in Disneyland
imagining myself living
as the young princess heroines,
aspiring to be brave, plucky
and above all else, devoted
to the gold-hearted prince
and tolerant of his beastly flaws.

But Prince Charming was never
your personal masculine model;
not even haughty Gaston caught
your young admiring imagination.
Tyler Durden wasn't much for flowers
and after all Trinity had to die tragically
for Neo to win as the lone hero in the end.

Serpents

Doting parents
drop serpents
into every crib.

The slitherers
stay invisible
growing fat
on blue shame
schooled cruelty
all the terrors
people plant
for the sake
of purity
vigilance
obedience
toughness.

They grow
into dragons
drinking tears
we quietly weep
in the chilly night.

They're vast
as empires
stronger than
nightmares
blood cold as
underfed souls.

I wish I could slay
the serpent that's
whispering you're
forever broken
a fraud
a mistake
unworthy of love.

But all I have is
this stupid pen
and it is not
mightier.

But maybe
if the dragons
won't let us love
our flawed selves
we can still love
one other
as hard
as we
can.

Mythical

The immortal Greek king
stands in a cool pool
of refreshing water
cursed to flee his lips.

Meanwhile, a plain girl
in deep, shunned shade
sits by the playground
watching pretty kids play.

"You can't be thirsty,"
Hades tells the king.
"The water's right here;
perhaps you aren't trying."

The girl knows she's fat,
her clothes dorky, old,
her glasses nerd-thick;
the kids have told her so.

"You can't possibly be lonely
with so many classmates,"
her mom remarks at breakfast.
"I had lots of friends at your age."

"Eat your waffles," her father says.
"You think you have problems?
The receptionist the agency sent
is the fattest whale you ever saw."

The girl doesn't remind him that
on the receptionist's first day,
school let out early for Easter
and so she walked to his office.

The new receptionist was reading
a Wonder Woman comic and greeted
the girl like a friend. And they chatted
about Amazons, heroes and gorgons.

"Can she type?" her mom asks.
"Who cares if she can type?" he says.
"I'm running a business, not SeaWorld.
Customers run from a face like hers."

The shaded girl opens her backpack:
there's the sack of colorful plastic snakes
her mom wouldn't buy at the dollar store:
"Those are ugly, and they're for boys!"

So, when nobody was looking,
she shoved it under her sweatshirt
next to her hammering heart
and walked out, head high.

She winds the vinyl serpents
into her hair like daisies,
jumps up and lunges
at the kids, hissing

into each frightened face
to respect the goddess
or else her vengeance
shall turn them all to stone.

She's hauled off
to the principal's office
and he asks her: "Why?"
But she is proudly silent.

Her parents fuss, but it's fine.
Detention doesn't hurt
any worse than mirrors;
she can steal more snakes
to keep for the next time.

Part Four:
Final Frontiers

When the War Ended

We brought home live prizes:
the greatest, coldest minds
set them in perfect suburbia
and put them to work
on our rocketing future.

Our sanitized monsters watched on high
as unsung black women worked geometry
to create a perfect white combat field
in the darkness of the 238,900 miles
between us and our great silver target.

The war was fought with television,
slide rules, and a sea of kerosene,
no guns, so Armstrong's conscience
was clear as he touched the plaque
that said we came in peace.

Mission Commander's Log

They put us through
hours of psych tests
for stellar reasons.
They want cleverness,
solid problem-solving,
bravery ever tempered
by a powerful will to live.

They do not value
emotion of any sort,
nor great imagination
(though it tangos hand-
in-hand with intellect).

They want a mind
relentlessly focused
on the job at hand:
burn rate, trajectories,
the calculus of survival
in a harsh freezing vacuum.

They do not want a brain
that wanders by mistake
peering into infinite dark,
scrying the devourers
lying in wait at the cores
of Canes Venatici or Cepheus.

Communion with the Void
paralyzes the soul
and with it the hand
and heroes must maintain
fast angular momentum.

Navigational Error

All my gold-plated intentions
mean an empty sector nothing
in the face of shattered helmets,
perfectly spherical ruby droplets
misting, glittering in our shared air.

Hyperfocus is good for astrophysics,
great for some brave rocket race
where cold equations rule the day
and emotions are for orphans
left squinting into blank skies.

There's no solid telemetry
to predict the arcing crash
of your plummeting trust.
No math for the fracture
of a single human heart.

You burn like the Pistol Star:
bright, fierce, entirely justified
you could have left me adrift
in blackout radio silence
lost to cosmic dust.

The truth is your radiation
is a gift precious as palladium;
you could have gone hypernova
but you haven't thrown me from orbit
and that means we see a fresh dawn.

Shore Leave

Months on Mars lugging steel plates
earn me only minutes on my knees
braced on the cool Earthbound sheets
before my muscles burn and shake.

I vainly wish for the resiliency
we all had back at the Academy
but my head wasn't strong enough
to take this dark room exposure

and his heart wasn't tall enough
to see past the barrel of his rocket
and she was premed and pre-meds
a strict comet beyond anyone's orbit.

Our aged images might shatter lenses
but back in the day, we couldn't appreciate
this tangled napping, gravitational bodies
cozy, floating in each other's dreams.

Dirty Americans

After years of hippie locks
you buzzed your scalp short.
I was obsessed with the fuzz.

Rubbing your stubble escalated
tensions in our situation room
and soon your face was between

my thighs, and I liked the look
of it there, as if some grizzled
general was kneeling to serve

my purple valley's majesty.
Aw yeah baby bend that massive
military-industrial-Phaeton complex

to my moist monomaniacal pleasures;
tap Morse code upon my eager flesh:
billion-dollar budgets, body counts.

Inject Edex into that flagging recruitment
campaign and tell me about the rocket race
that'll shoot us far past Venus and Mars.

Promise me that after all this aggression,
all this leather-harnessed patriarchy,
we'll finally come in peace.

November 28, 2120

These cranberries never
graced a Massachusetts bog
and frankly, they're mostly
rice syrup and cochineal.
This extruded protein loaf
only faintly resembles
an authentic turkey roast
but half the ship's crew
are vegetarians anyhow
and just this morning
we spied the first light
shining blue and brave
off the rolling oceans
of our brand new home
so we could be feasting
upon autoclaved dirt
and today I'd still
be thankful.

Dawn

The rare instance
when you awaken
simply a human
on cool, soft sheets
not a floundering father
nor a mother frantically late
nor a solitary disappointment
to bosses, friends or yourself.

Yourself.

In that moment,
you're only just

Yourself.

Who is this mystery?
This person unburdened
from deadlines and fears?
Who is this soul feeling
a heartbeat's freedom?

Unbound, do you float
clear into outer space
identity and purpose
nothing but mist?

Or is there another you
occupying your body
a comfortable friend
a steadfast anchor
to the beautiful world
gently whispering *Hey*
the day's just begun.

Publication History

"Faith" – *Chiral Mad 5,* Written Backwards, August 2021.

"At the Downtown University" – *Chiral Mad 5,* Written Backwards, August 2021.

"Dawn" – *Like Sunshine After Rain,* Raw Dog Screaming Press, July 2021.

"Fragile" – *Weirdbook #44,* 2020.

"It Only Hurts When I Dream" – *Tales of the Lost 3,* Plaid Dragon Press, 2021.

"October" – *Tales of the Lost 2,* Plaid Dragon Press, October 2020.

"Silences" – *Vastarien: A Literary Journal,* Summer 2019.

"bad night" – *Weirdbook #39,* July 2018.

"Salty" – *Weirdbook Annual #1,* October 2017.

"November" – *The Fat Damsel,* August 2017.

"The Wrong Daughter" – *Weirdbook #34,* February 2017.

"Shore Leave" – *Illumen,* Autumn 2016.

"The Scientist's Paramour" – *Asimov's Science Fiction Magazine,* October/November 2016.

"Scary" – *Scary Out There,* Simon & Schuster Books For Young Readers, August 2016.

"Dangerous" – *Scary Out There,* Simon & Schuster Books For Young Readers, August 2016.

"turnt" – *Scary Out There,* Simon & Schuster Books For Young Readers, August 2016.

"Wolf Waltz" – HWA Poetry Showcase Vol. III, August 2016.

"Employee Recognition Day" – *Star*Line,* Summer 2016.

"February" – *The Pitkin Review,* June 2016.

"Recreation" – *The Cutting Room,* Tachyon Publications, October 2014. First appeared in *A Sea of Alone: Poems for Alfred Hitchcock,* Dark Scribe Press, July 2011

"The Unforgiving King" – *Haiku Cthulhu,* Pulse Publishing, April 2021..

Acknowledgements

I'd like to thank my Patreon supporters who helped make this book possible:

Abyss & Apex Magazine
Amanda Hoffelt-Ryan
Amy Estes
Anita Siraki
Anne Marie Lutz
Anthony Klancar
Anthony R. Cardno
Arasibo Campeche
Benjamin Holesapple
Brit Marshalk
Carie Martin
Cody Nowack
Dan Stout
David Wyatt
Deanne Fountaine
Donna Munro
Dora Knez
Elizabeth Bennefeld
Elizabeth Donald
Eric Grizzle
Eric Sprague
Evan Dicken
Ferrett Steinmetz
Hanna Brady
Heather Ross
Holly Zaldivar
Human People
Ingrid de Beus
J. Thorne
James A. McCoy
Jamie Milhoan
Jeanna Tendean
jennifer Covel
Jennifer Liles
Jim Leach
Joe and Gay Haldeman
Joe Mynhardt
Joel Kramer
Julie Megchelsen
Karen Engelsen
Kari Wolfe
Kira Barnes
Laurel Halbany
Laurent Castellucci

Linda Addison
Lisa Morton
Lorena Haldeman
Margaret Steurer
Mark Freeman
Martha Wells
Michael Cieslak
Michael Mock
Molly DePriest
Rebecca J. Allred
Rob Funk
Roberta Slocumb
Rona Gofstein
Sara Marks
Sarah Hans
Sarah Page
Sarah Walker
Scott A. Johnson
Scott Slemmons
Shannon Eichorn
Stephanie Heminger
Tom Smith
Tonya Liburd
Weston Kincade

About the Author

Lucy A. Snyder is the Shirley Jackson Award-nominated and five-time Bram Stoker Award-winning author of 15 books. Her most recent titles are the short story collection *Halloween Season* and the forthcoming novel *Apocalypse Apocrypha.* Her first poetry collection, *Chimeric Machines*, won the Stoker. Over 50 of her poems have appeared in publications such as *Asimov's Science Fiction, Weirdbook, Vastarien*, and *Nightmare Magazine*. She lives in Columbus, Ohio with a small jungle of houseplants, a clowder of cats, and an insomnia of housemates. You can learn more about her at www.lucysnyder.com and you can follow her on Twitter at @LucyASnyder.

CPSIA information can be obtained
at www.ICGtesting.com
Printed in the USA
BVHW071345070721
611307BV00002B/165